Quotations of Barack Obama

2004 - 2017

BANTRY BAY PUBLISHING
CHICAGO

Hope Democracy Change

Tolerance Compassion Perseverance

Civil Rights Courage Respect

Grace Justice

Unity Diversity

Strength Love

Family *Freedom*

Immigration Racial Equality

Dignity Optimism Activism

Marriage Equality Truth Women

Yes, We Can.

Quotations of Barack Obama

Of the nearly 150 quotations included in this book, many were spoken at significant moments in our nation's history, moments etched in our minds, moments when Mr. Obama's voice was most needed. Many of those are indexed below. A full reader's guide to his quotations can be found on pages 110 and 111.

Preface

This compilation of quotations is a tribute to Barack Obama, the 44th President of the United States of America and his eight transformative years in office. These eloquent words can forever serve as confirmation of what he brought to the Oval Office: dignity, brilliance, strength, grace and an open heart.

A gifted writer and speaker, the President understood the power of language and deployed it with an elegance and style unsurpassed by any who have held the office.

As you page through these quotations, you'll be reminded of the markers he laid for social and economic justice, his fervent protection of, and advocacy for, democracy, and his beliefs that hope is eternal and that change is the product of passion, dedication and clear-eyed commitment.

My heart is filled with love for this country.

October 17, 2006 *Excerpt from* The Audacity of Hope:
Thoughts on Reclaiming the American Dream
Crown Publishing

July 27, 2004 *Candidate for U.S. Senate in Illinois, Barack Obama, delivered the keynote address at the Democratic National Convention in Boston. It was described in* The Washington Post *as "The 17 minutes that launched a political star."*

2004

Hope in the face of difficulty, hope in the face of uncertainty, the audacity of hope: In the end, that is God's greatest gift to us, the bedrock of this nation, a belief in things not seen, a belief that there are better days ahead.

I stand here knowing that my story is part of the larger American story, that I owe a debt to all of those who came before me, and that in no other country on earth is my story even possible.

There is not a liberal America and a conservative America — there is the United States of America. There is not a Black America and a White America and Latino America and Asian America — there's the United States of America.

July 27, 2004 *Excerpts from speech to the Democratic National Convention*

2004

It is that fundamental belief — I am my brother's keeper, I am my sister's keeper — that makes this country safe.

Do we participate in a politics of cynicism, or do we participate in a politics of hope?

July 27, 2004 *Excerpts from speech to the Democratic National Convention*

2005

Focusing your life solely on making a buck shows a certain poverty of ambition. It asks too little of yourself ... Because it's only when you hitch your wagon to something larger than yourself that you realize your true potential.

June 4, 2005 *Knox College Commencement*
Galesburg, Illinois

2006

Issues are never simple. One thing I'm proud of is that very rarely will you hear me simplify the issues.

September 25, 2006 *MSNBC interview*

I'm inspired by my own children, how full they make my heart. They make me want to work to make the world a little bit better. And they make me want to be a better man.

October 17, 2006 *Excerpt from* The Audacity of Hope: Thoughts on Reclaiming the American Dream *Crown Publishing*

2006

My little girls can break my heart. They can make me cry just looking at them eating their string beans.

October 29, 2006 *Remarks in Austin, Texas, about the importance of balancing family life with politics*

2007

A change in our politics can only come from you, from people across our country who believe there's a better way and are willing to work for it … So even in the midst of the enormous challenges we face today, I have great faith and hope about the future — because I believe in you.

January 16, 2007 *Presidential exploratory announcement*

February 10, 2007 *Springfield, Illinois*

2007

It was here [Springfield] where we learned to disagree without being disagreeable; that it's possible to compromise so long as you know those principles that can never be compromised; and that so long as we're willing to listen to each other, we can assume the best in people instead of the worst.

In the shadow of the Old State Capitol, where Lincoln once called on a house divided to stand together, where common hopes and common dreams still live, I stand before you today to announce my candidacy for President of the United States of America.

So let us begin. Let us begin this hard work together. Let us transform this nation.

February 10, 2007 *Springfield, Illinois*

2007

Torture and secrecy betray core American values. Torture is how you create enemies, not how you defend them.

2007 *Campaign press release*

One of the things I think I can bring to the presidency is to make government and public service cool again.

November 2007 Time *magazine interview*

2008

The truth is, actually, words do inspire. Words do help people get involved ... Don't discount that power. Because when the American people determine that something is going to happen, then it happens.

> **January 5, 2008** *Excerpt of comments made during a debate with Hillary Clinton*

I will never forget that the only reason I'm standing here today is because somebody, somewhere stood up for me when it was risky. Stood up when it was hard. Stood up when it wasn't popular. And because that somebody stood up, a few more stood up. And then a few thousand stood up. And then a few million stood up. And standing up, with courage and clear purpose, they somehow managed to change the world.

> **January 8, 2008** *Nashua, New Hampshire*

Quotations of Barack Obama

2008

True unity cannot be so easily purchased. It starts with a change in attitudes. It starts with changing our hearts, and changing our minds, broadening our spirit.

I talk about hope. I talk about it a lot because the odds of me standing here today are so small, so remote that I couldn't have gotten here without some hope ... I wasn't born into money, or great wealth, or great privilege, or status. I was given love, an education, and some hope. That's what I got.

In the struggle to heal this nation and repair the world, we cannot walk alone. So I ask you to walk with me and march with me and join your voices with mine, and together we will sing the song that tears down the walls that divide us and lift up an America that is truly indivisible with liberty and justice for all.

January 20, 2008 *Excerpts of address at Ebenezer Baptist Church in Atlanta, Georgia*

2008

I chose to run for President at this moment in history because I believe deeply that we cannot solve the challenges of our time unless we solve them together, unless we perfect our union by understanding that we may have different stories, but we hold common hopes.

This union may never be perfect, but generation after generation has shown that it can always be perfected. And today, whenever I find myself feeling doubtful or cynical about this possibility, what gives me the most hope is the next generation, the young people whose attitudes and beliefs and openness to change have already made history in this election.

March 18, 2008 *"A More Perfect Union" speech in Philadelphia, Pennsylvania*

2008

Of all the rocks upon which we build our lives, we are reminded today that family is the most important.

June 15, 2008 *Senator Barack Obama's remarks at the Apostolic Church of God in Chicago*

2008

Let our children come here, and know this history, so that they can add their voices to proclaim 'never again.'

July 23, 2008 *Excerpt from his entry into the guest book at Yad Vashem Holocaust Memorial in Jerusalem, Israel*

2008

The best judge of whether or not a country is going to develop, is how it treats its women. If it's educating its girls, if women have equal rights, that country is going to move forward. But if women are oppressed and abused and illiterate, then they're going to fall behind.

September 2008 Ladies' Home Journal *feature*

If I had to name my greatest strength, I guess it would be my humility. Greatest weakness? It's possible that I'm a little too awesome.

October 16, 2008 *Alfred E. Smith Memorial Foundation Dinner at the Waldorf Astoria Hotel in New York City*

2008

If there is anyone out there who still doubts that America is a place where all things are possible, who still wonders if the dream of our founders is alive in our time, who still questions the power of our democracy, tonight is your answer.

I will never forget who this victory truly belongs to. It belongs to you.

November 4, 2008 *Grant Park, Chicago Victory Speech*

2008

Tonight, we have proved once more that the true strength of our nation comes not from the might of our arms, or the scale of our wealth, but from the enduring power of our ideals: democracy, liberty, opportunity, and unyielding hope.

This is our moment. This is our time ... And where we are met with cynicism and doubt and those who tell us that we can't, we will respond with that timeless creed that sums up the spirit of a people: Yes, we can.

November 4, 2008 *Grant Park, Chicago Victory Speech*

NEW YORK POST ELECTION 2008 SPECIAL · LATE CITY FINAL

OBAMA'S HISTORIC VICTORY

MR. PRESIDENT

LEXINGTON · HERALD-LEADER ELECTION 2008

YES, HE CAN: OBAMA WINS

FIRST BLACK PRESIDENT

McCONNELL RE-ELECTED
Senator now becomes nation's top Republican

SPECIAL ELECTION EDITION: 16 PAGES OF COVERAGE

GOV. DANIELS CRUISES TO 2ND TERM

THE INDIANAPOLIS STAR

HISTORY

OBAMA ELECTED NATION'S 1ST BLACK PRESIDENT

'Nationwide gains expand Democrats' control of House and Senate'

'This is a big day for change,' Obama's victory proves

AT THIS DEFINING MOMENT, CHANGE HAS COME TO AMERICA

The Times-Picayune

THE 44th PRESIDENT

IN HISTORIC RUN, OBAMA WINS WHITE HOUSE

Lorraine wins a third term

Scalise wins 1st District

Jefferson beats Moreno

THE COMMERCIAL APPEAL

YES HE DID

HISTORY | Democrat Barack Obama becomes first black man to be elected president
NEXT STEP | Tells thousands gathered to celebrate in Chicago that 'change has come'

ELECTION EDITION

Portland Press Herald

OBAMA SURGES TO HISTORIC WIN

Defying GOP slide, Collins is re-elected

The Democrat scores a convincing win as voters hungry for change elect the first black U.S. president

---

The Detroit News

"A new dawn of American leadership is at hand."

OBAMA STEPS INTO HISTORY

Dramatic victory puts African American in White House for first time and puts Democrats in firm control of power after eight years of Republican rule

---

The Clarion-Ledger

PRESIDENT OBAMA

'THE DREAM OF OUR FOUNDERS IS ALIVE'

Wicker leads Musgrove, who waits for final count

Obama sweeps to victory as first black president

ELECTION 2008 ★ 20 PAGES OF COVERAGE INSIDE

The Providence Journal

Democrat wins popular, electoral votes

PRESIDENT OBAMA

U.S. overwhelmingly elects first black president

Family pauses in welcome history

CHICAGO SUN-TIMES

MR. PRESIDENT

THE BALTIMORE SUN
WEDNESDAY 11.5.2008

It's Obama

Democrat gains historic victory, will be the nation's first black president

Md. voters give Ok to 15,000 slots

GOVERNOR: Congdon retains victory in close race with Rossi

A new American majority takes shape

THE NEWS TRIBUNE

TheNewsTribune.com

'CHANGE HAS COME'

OBAMA CALLS FOR 'NEW SPIRIT OF PATRIOTISM'

COUNTY EXECUTIVE Winner a trump as county debate ended with voter outcry

HUGE TURNOUT: Pierce County voters wait in long lines

U.S. PRESIDENT: Popular vote close, but McCain loses key states

---

StarTribune

StarTribune.com

OBAMA

Supporters are euphoric as he promises era of change

Bitter Senate race between Coleman, Franken too close to call

2009

Throughout America's history, there have been some years that simply rolled into the next without much notice or fanfare. And then there are the years that come along once in a generation, the kind that mark a clean break from a troubled past and set a new course for our nation. This is one of those years.

January 8, 2009 *Financial Crisis Address at George Mason University in Fairfax, Virginia*

2009

There is no doubt that our road will be long, that our climb will be steep. But never forget that the true character of our nation is revealed not during times of comfort and ease, but by the right we do when the moment is hard.

January 18, 2009 *Pre-Inauguration address at the Lincoln Memorial*

2009

Starting today, we must pick ourselves up, dust ourselves off, and begin again the work of remaking America.

Let it be said by our children's children that when we were tested, we refused to let this journey end, that we did not turn back, nor did we falter; and eyes fixed on the horizon and God's grace upon us, we carried forth that great gift of freedom and delivered it safely to future generations.

January 20, 2009 *Inaugural Address*

January 20, 2009 *Oath of office*

2009

It is fitting that with the very first bill I sign, we are upholding one of this nation's first principles: that we are all created equal and each deserve a chance to pursue our own version of happiness.

Equal pay isn't just an economic issue for millions of Americans and their families, it's a question of who we are — and whether we're truly living up to our fundamental ideals.

January 29, 2009 *Lilly Ledbetter Fair Pay Restoration Act signing*

The strongest democracies flourish from frequent and lively debate, but they endure when people of every background and belief find a way to set aside smaller differences in service of a greater purpose.

February 9, 2009 *White House press conference*

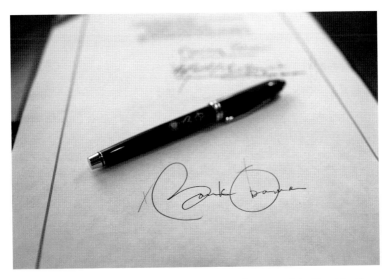

February 17, 2009 *Aboard Air Force One, a close-up of the President's signature on the American Recovery and Reinvestment Act, which he had just signed in Denver. (Official White House photo by Pete Souza)*

2009

Don't shortchange the future because of fear in the present.

April 1, 2009 *Joint News Conference with British Prime Minister Gordon Brown in London*

2009

True peace is not just freedom from fear, but freedom from want.

The absence of hope can rot a society from within.

Let us reach for the world that ought to be — that spark of the divine that still stirs within each of our souls.

December 10, 2009 *Nobel Lecture, Oslo City Hall, Norway*

December 10, 2009
President Obama looks at the Nobel Peace Prize medal at the Nobel Institute in Oslo, Norway.

(Official White House photo by Pete Souza)

2010

Yes, we're passing through a hard winter. It's the hardest in some time. But let's always remember that, as a people, the American people, we've weathered some hard winters before. And yet, each season, the frost melts, the cold recedes, the sun reappears. So it was for earlier generations, and so it will be for us.

Sometimes, it's hard to be a good father and good mother. Sometimes, it's hard to be a good neighbor, or a good citizen, to give up time in service of others, to give something of ourselves to a cause greater than ourselves.

There are times when I'm not so calm. There are times when progress seems too slow. There are times when the words that are spoken about me hurt. There are times when the barbs sting. There are times when it feels like all these efforts are for naught … During those times, it's faith that keeps me calm. It's faith that gives me peace.

January 17, 2010 *Martin Luther King, Jr. Remembrance Speech*

2011

We may have differences in policy, but we all believe in the rights enshrined in our Constitution. We may have different opinions, but we believe in the same promise that says this is a place where you can make it if you try. We may have different backgrounds, but we believe in the same dream that says this is a country where anything's possible. No matter who you are. No matter where you come from.

January 25, 2011 *Excerpt from the State of the Union Address*

2011

And where is the NPR table? You guys are still here? That's good. I couldn't remember where we landed on that. Now, I know you were a little tense when the GOP tried to cut your funding, but personally, I was looking forward to new programming like 'No Things Considered' or 'Wait, Wait … Don't Fund Me.'

April 30, 2011 *White House Correspondents' Association Dinner at the Hilton Hotel in Washington, D.C.*

2011

Tonight, we are once again reminded that America can do whatever we set our mind to. That is the story of our history, whether it's the pursuit of prosperity for our people, or the struggle for equality for all our citizens; our commitment to stand up for our values abroad, and our sacrifices to make the world a safer place.

May 1, 2011 *President Obama announces the death of Osama bin Laden. Below, the President and members of the national security team receive an update on the mission against bin Laden in the Situation Room of the White House. (Official White House photo by Pete Souza)*

My name is Barack Obama of the Moneygall
Obamas, and I've come home to find the apostrophe that we
lost somewhere along the way.

May 23, 2011 *Excerpt from speech at Trinity College, Dublin, Ireland*

May 23, 2011 *President Obama talks with pub-goers as
pub owner and distant relative Ollie Hayes shows First Lady
Michelle Obama how to draw a pint in Moneygall, Ireland.
(Official White House photo by Pete Souza)*

June 9, 2011 *As the President was leaving the fourth grade closing ceremony for his daughter Sasha at her school in Bethesda, Maryland, he noticed some pre-school children peering out of a window at an adjacent child care facility, so he walked over to say hello to them. (Official White House photo by Pete Souza)*

2011

The future rewards those who press on. I don't have time to feel sorry for myself. I don't have time to complain. I'm going to press on.

> **September 24, 2011** *The Congressional Black Caucus Foundation Annual Phoenix Awards Dinner*

2011

I hate following Michelle. See, for you men out there who are not yet married, let me explain: The whole goal is to marry up — to try to improve your gene pool.

October 19, 2011 *Taking the podium after a speech by Michelle Obama at the Joint Base Langley-Eustis in Hampton, Virginia*

2012

When I think about this boy, I think about my own kids. You know, if I had a son, he'd look like Trayvon.

All of us have to do some soul searching to figure out how does something like this happen.

> **March 23, 2012** *Remarks at the White House following the shooting death of 17-year-old Trayvon Martin*

April 18, 2012 *President Obama sits in the famous Rosa Parks bus at the Henry Ford Museum after an event in Dearborn, Michigan. Ms. Parks was arrested sitting in the same row Mr. Obama is in, but on the opposite side. (Official White House photo by Pete Souza)*

2012

We know we are better off when women are treated fairly and equally in every aspect of American life, whether it's the salary you earn or the health decisions you make.

May 14, 2012 *Keynote address at Barnard College's 120th Commencement ceremony in New York City*

December 14, 2012 *President Obama wipes away a tear as he delivers a statement on the mass shooting at Sandy Hook Elementary School in Newtown, Connecticut. (Official White House photo by Pete Souza)*

2012

Our hearts are broken today for the parents and grandparents, sisters and brothers of these little children, and for the families of the adults who were lost. Our hearts are broken for the parents of the survivors as well, for as blessed as they are to have their children home tonight, they know that their children's innocence has been torn away from them too early, and there are no words that will ease their pain.

December 14, 2012 *A portion of the President's statement a few hours after 20 children between six and seven years old, as well as six adult staff members, were killed at the Sandy Hook Elementary School in Newtown, Connecticut*

This is our first task — caring for our children. It's our first job. If we don't get that right, we don't get anything right. That's how, as a society, we will be judged.

December 16, 2012 *Remarks at the Sandy Hook prayer vigil*

January 20, 2013 *Chief Justice John Roberts administers the oath of office to President Barack Obama during the official swearing-in ceremony in the Blue Room of the White House on Inauguration Day. First Lady Michelle Obama, holding the Robinson family Bible, and daughters Malia and Sasha, stand with the President.*
(Official White House photo by Lawrence Jackson)

2013

Progress does not compel us to settle centuries-long debates about the role of government for all time, but it does require us to act in our time.

For our journey is not complete until our wives, our mothers and daughters can earn a living equal to their efforts.

January 21, 2013 *Inaugural Address, Washington, D.C.*

2013

Reading is important. If you know how to read, then the whole world opens up to you.

April 1, 2013 *Comment by the President as he read "Chicka Chicka Boom Boom" to children at the White House Easter Egg Roll*

April 18, 2013 *President Obama delivers remarks at "Healing Our City: An Interfaith Service" dedicated to those who were gravely wounded or killed in the bombings near the finish line of the 2013 Boston Marathon.*

(WhiteHouse.gov)

2013

A celebration became a tragedy. And so we come together to pray, and mourn, and measure our loss. But we also come together to reclaim that state of grace — to reaffirm that the spirit of this city is undaunted, and the spirit of this country shall remain undimmed.

You've shown us, Boston, that in the face of evil, Americans will lift up what's good. In the face of cruelty, we will choose compassion. We'll choose friendship. We'll choose love.

Tomorrow, the sun will rise over Boston. Tomorrow, the sun will rise over this country that we love. This special place. This state of grace.

April 18, 2013 *Excerpts from the Boston Interfaith Service*

2013

The arc of the moral universe may bend towards justice, but it doesn't bend on its own.

August 28, 2013 *50th anniversary of the March on Washington, D.C.*

2013

Those of us who have the privilege to serve this country have an obligation to do our job as best we can. We come from different parties, but we are Americans first. And that's why disagreement cannot mean dysfunction. It can't degenerate into hatred. The American people's hopes and dreams are what matters, not ours.

October 17, 2013 *Remarks on the reopening of the government*

2014

The debate is settled. Climate change is a fact, and when our children's children look us in the eye and ask if we did all we could to leave them a safer, more stable world, with new sources of energy, I want us to say yes, we did.

January 28, 2014 *State of the Union*

2014

When women succeed, America succeeds.

When any of our citizens can't fulfill their potential for reasons that have nothing to do with their talent or their character or their work ethic, we're not living up to founding values.

Equal pay is not just an economic issue for millions of Americans and their families. It's also about whether we're willing to build an economy that works for everybody, and whether we're going to do our part to make sure that our daughters have the same chances to pursue their dreams as our sons, and whether or not we're willing to restore that basic idea: You can make it, no matter who you are, if you try.

April 8, 2014 *Equal Pay for Equal Work Remarks*

July 21, 2014 *President Obama and Vice President Joe Biden share a laugh in the Oval Office. (Official White House photo by Pete Souza)*

September 23, 2014 *President Obama, with First Lady Michelle Obama, delivers remarks during a United Nations reception at the Waldorf Astoria Hotel in New York City. (Official White House photo by Pete Souza)*

October 8, 2014 *President Barack Obama listens during a technology strategy discussion in the Rose Garden of the White House.*
(Official White House photo by Pete Souza)

2015

A woman's ability to decide how many children
to have and when, without interference from the government,
is one of the most fundamental rights we possess.

January 20, 2015 *State of the Union Address*

2015

Selma shows us that America is not the project of any one person. Because the single-most powerful word in our democracy is the word 'We.' 'We the People.' 'We Shall Overcome.' 'Yes, We Can.' That word is owned by no one. It belongs to everyone. Oh, what a glorious task we are given, to continually try to improve this great nation of ours.

March 7, 2015 *Selma Voting Rights March Commemoration Speech*

March 7, 2015 *President Obama and First Lady Michelle Obama join hands with Representative John Lewis, D-Georgia. The walk across the Edmund Pettus Bridge in Selma, Alabama commemorated the 50th Anniversary of Bloody Sunday and the Selma-to-Montgomery civil rights marches. Malia and Sasha Obama join hands with their grandmother, Marian Robinson. (Official White House photo by Lawrence Jackson)*

March 27, 2015 *The First Couple share a tender moment before a video recording for the 2015 World Expo, in the Diplomatic Reception Room of the White House. (Official White House photo by Pete Souza)*

April 5, 2015 *The President, First Lady, and daughters Malia and Sasha pose for a family portrait with Bo and Sunny in the Rose Garden of the White House on Easter Sunday.*

(Official White House photo by Pete Souza)

2015

Six years into my presidency, some people still say
I'm arrogant, aloof, condescending. Some people are so dumb.

April 25, 2015 *White House Correspondents' Association
Dinner at the Hilton Hotel in Washington, D.C.*

*President Barack Obama delivers remarks with the help of
his "anger translator," comedic actor Keegan-Michael Key.
(Official White House photo by Lawrence Jackson)*

June 18, 2015 *The President speaks at a DNC fundraiser hosted by Tyler Perry at his Los Angeles home.   (Photograph by Lisa Green)*

June 25, 2015 *The President reacts after an aide interrupted a meeting to inform him that the Supreme Court had affirmed the Affordable Care Act subsidies ruling.*

(Official White House photo by Pete Souza)

2015

Today, we can say in no uncertain terms that we've made our Union a little more perfect.

Love is love.

> **June 26, 2015** *Remarks after the U.S. Supreme Court legalized same-sex marriage*

June 26, 2015 *President Obama led a congregation of 5,500 in singing "Amazing Grace" during the eulogy for Reverend Clementa Pinckney. Reverend Pinckney was one of nine people killed in a shooting at the Emanuel AME Church in Charleston, South Carolina. Mr. Obama's eulogy has been widely acknowledged as one of the most powerful moments of his presidency.*

I've had to make statements like this too many times. Communities have had to endure tragedies like this too many times ... And it is in our power to do something about it.

June 18, 2015 *Remarks at a White House press briefing after the President received word of the Charleston murders*

This whole week, I've been reflecting on this idea of grace. The grace of the families who lost loved ones. The grace that Reverend Pinckney would preach about in his sermons. The grace described in one of my favorite hymns — the one we all know. Amazing grace, how sweet the sound that saved a wretch like me. I once was lost, but now I'm found; was blind but now I see.

By recognizing our common humanity, by treating every child as important, regardless of the color of their skin or the station into which they were born, and to do what's necessary to make opportunity real for every American — by doing that, we express God's grace.

June 26, 2015 *Remarks at the memorial service for Reverend Clementa Pinckney and eight other shooting victims*

2015

I refuse to stop fighting now. For the sake of my daughters and yours, we must do better to make sure women are respected and treated equally.

August 18, 2015 *95th anniversary of the 19th Amendment, the amendment which gave women the right to vote*

October 23, 2015 *Afternoon autumn light bathes the President as he works at the Resolute Desk in the Oval Office. (Official White House photo by Pete Souza)*

2016

We need to reject any politics that target people because of race or religion. This isn't a matter of political correctness. It's a matter of understanding what makes us strong.

When you come after Americans, we go after you. It may take time, but we have long memories, and our reach has no limits.

January 12, 2016 *The State of the Union Address*

February 18, 2016 *After President Obama spoke at a White House reception celebrating African American History Month, this little boy waited in awe as the President greeted audience members on the rope line. Photographer Pete Souza snapped this photo just before the President bent down to talk with the boy. Afterwards, Souza tracked down his name—Clark Reynolds—and had the President sign a copy for him. Notice the position of the boy's necktie.*

(Official White House Photo by Pete Souza)

2016

I tease Joe sometimes, but he has been at my side for seven years. I love that man. He's not just a great vice president, he's a great friend. We've gotten so close that in some places in Indiana, they won't serve us pizza.

In my final year, my approval ratings keep going up. The last time I was this high, I was trying to decide on my major.

Obama out.

April 30, 2016 *White House Correspondents' Association Dinner at the Hilton Hotel in Washington, D.C.*

2016

Have confidence in your legacy. Have confidence in your blackness.

May 7, 2016 *Howard University Commencement*

Progress doesn't travel a straight line, but instead zigs and zags, in fits and starts.

May 15, 2016 *Rutgers University Commencement*

2016

Those who died, they are like us. Ordinary people understand this, I think. They do not want more war. They would rather that the wonders of science be focused on improving life and not eliminating it. When the choices made by nations, when the choices made by leaders, reflect this simple wisdom, then the lesson of Hiroshima is done.

May 27, 2016 *Excerpt of remarks at Hiroshima, Japan*

2016

... the Black Lives Matter movement has been hugely important in getting all of America to see the challenges in the criminal justice system differently. And I could not be prouder of the activism that has been involved. And it's making a difference.

I think of myself as a relay runner ... Sometimes, you take the baton and you're behind in the race, and you've got to run a little bit harder to catch up. Hopefully, by the time you pass on the baton, you're a little bit better positioned in the race. And I think there is a humility that comes out of this office, because you feel that no matter how much you've done, there's more work to do.

But I think that there is a confidence that well-meaning people working together can change the country for the better. I've seen it happen.

July 1, 2016 *Interview with Steve Inskeep of NPR*

2016

I do think that, in that sense of what is true for a lot of African American men, is there's a greater presumption of dangerousness that arises from the social and cultural perceptions that have been fed to folks for a long time.

In the end, it's not about finding policies that work; it's about forging consensus and fighting cynicism and finding the will to make change.

July 12, 2016 *Memorial Service for five Dallas police officers*

My hope is, that out of the tragedies that happened ... we are able to see each other as one family, that the mom of a police officer who is killed and the mom of an individual who is killed by a police officer, they have both lost a son.

July 14, 2016 *Town Hall: The President and the People:*
A National Conversation

2004 - 2017

2016

America isn't about 'yes he will.' It's about 'yes we can.'

You've picked me up. I hope sometimes I picked you up, too.

Show the world we still believe in the promise of this great nation.

July 27, 2016 *Address at the Democratic National Convention*

2016

... It is so important today that we reaffirm our character as a nation — a people drawn from every corner of the world, every color, every religion, every background — bound by a creed as old as our founding, e pluribus unum. Out of many, we are one.

For we know that our diversity — our patchwork heritage — is not a weakness; it is still, and always will be, one of our greatest strengths. This is the America that was attacked that September morning. This is the America that we must remain true to.

September 11, 2016 *Excerpt from remarks by President Obama to the survivors and families of 9/11 at a memorial service at the Pentagon*

2016

I do not believe progress is possible if our desire to preserve our identities gives way to an impulse to dehumanize or dominate another group. If our religions lead us to persecute those of another faith, if we jail or beat people who are gay, if our traditions lead us to prevent girls from going to school, if we discriminate on the basis of race, or tribe, or ethnicity, then the fragile bonds of civilizations will fray.

Today, a nation ringed by walls would only imprison itself.

September 20, 2016 *Excerpts from the President's final address to the United Nations General Assembly*

Quotations of Barack Obama

2016

A world in which one percent of humanity controls as much wealth as the other 99 percent will never be stable.

We need to follow through on our efforts to combat climate change … and only then can we continue lifting all people up from poverty without condemning our children to a planet beyond their capacity to repair.

We need to embrace the tolerance that results from respect of all human beings.

September 20, 2016 *Excerpts from the President's final address to the United Nations General Assembly*

2016 *A bedsheet banner displayed at The National Museum of African American History and Culture, a gift of Elizabeth Hess*

2016

This is the story of the African American experience. It is a story that is full of tragedy, but is also about great joy and great victories. It is a story that is not just a story of the past, but is alive and well today.

We're not a burden on America, or a stain on America, or an object of pity, or charity for America. We're America. And that's what this museum explains, the fact that our stories have shaped every corner of our culture …

Hopefully, this museum makes us talk to each other. And more importantly, listen to each other.

September 24, 2016 *Remarks at the National Museum of African American History and Culture*

2016

If we join hands, and we do things right, if we maintain our dignity, and we continue to appeal to the better angels of this nation, progress will be made.

I know that years from now, like all of you, Michelle and I will be able to come here to this museum and not just bring our kids, but hopefully our grandkids. I imagine holding a little hand of somebody and telling them the stories that are enshrined here.

September 24, 2016 *Remarks at the National Museum of African American History and Culture*

September 24, 2016 *Congressman John Lewis and President Barack Obama embrace at the dedication of the National Museum of African American History and Culture.*
(Photo by Leah L. Jones for the NMAAHC)

2016

Today is a historic day in the fight to protect our planet for future generations. Make no mistake: This agreement will help delay and avoid some of the worst consequences of climate change.

If we follow through on the commitments that this Paris Agreement embodies, history may well judge it as a turning point for our planet.

October 6, 2016 *Paris Agreement on Climate Change*

October 11, 2016 *President Obama promoting "www. mentor.gov," and "My Brother's Keeper" during ESPN's* The Undefeated: A Conversation with The President: Sports, Race and Achievement *at North Carolina A&T State University in Greensboro, North Carolina. He's shown above with moderator Stan Verrett of ESPN and alumnus Terrence J.*

2016

Understand the power of second chances and redemption … [as a kid] I made all kinds of bad decisions, so if that's true for me, it's true for kids everywhere.

How you do it [protest] is less important than your commitment to use whatever platforms you have to speak to not just issues of racial injustice, but to speak to issues of discrimination against Muslims, or sexual assault on college campuses, or a whole host of issues.

October 11, 2016 *Excerpts of remarks at North Carolina A&T State University in Greensboro, North Carolina*

2016

Innovation is in our DNA. Science has always been central to our progress.

We're the nation that just had six of our scientists and researchers win Nobel Prizes — and every one of them was an immigrant.

October 13, 2016 *Comments at the White House Frontiers Conference*

2016

This is the people's house, and it ought to reflect the amazing diversity, and the imagination, and the incredible ingenuity that defines the American people.

October 21, 2016 *Remarks at the BET White House musical celebration*

2016

There's no one who I believe has ever captured the soul of America more profoundly than Abraham Lincoln has. Somebody who was able to see humanity clearly, see the fundamental contradictions of the American experiment clearly, and yet still remain hopeful and still remain full of humor, and still have a basic sympathy for the human condition, even in the midst of a terrible war and having to make terrible decisions. And having a forgiving spirit.

I'm named Barack Hussein Obama. I'm African American. And I've been elected twice to this office with the majorities of the American people. So something is working.

Anybody who gets into bed and turns out the lights the first night in the White House, probably feels a little bit of a start, where you say, 'Goodness …'

November 2016 Vanity Fair *interview with Doris Kearns Goodwin*

2016

So there's a reason that I've got gray hair — because I've been busy.

You can't be against something. You've got to be for something.

I'm asking you the same thing I asked of you eight years ago. I'm asking you to believe … I'm asking you to believe in your ability to change things.

This is the moment we choose hope. Choose hope … We'll continue this amazing journey. We will finish what we started. We will show the world why America is the greatest nation on Earth.

November 4, 2016 *Excerpts from a campaign rally speech at Florida International University*

2016

Your job as a citizen and as a decent human being is to constantly affirm and lift up and fight for treating people with kindness and respect and understanding. And you should anticipate that at any given moment, there's going to be flare-ups of bigotry that you may have to confront, or may be inside you and you have to vanquish. And it doesn't stop ... You don't get into a fetal position about it. You don't start worrying about apocalypse. You say, 'O.K., where are the places where I can push to keep it moving forward?'

November 11, 2016 *Part of what the President told his daughters after the November 8th election (via* The New Yorker *and David Remnick).*

2016

The road ahead is certainly going to be bumpier than we expected. We can't get discouraged. We can't get cynical ... It's time to brush ourselves off, get back in the arena, and get ready to fight.

November 13, 2016 *Excerpt of President Obama's comments in an email to DNC supporters*

2016

The gift of democracy is ours, and ours alone, to nurture and protect.

November 24, 2016 *Thanksgiving Address to the nation*

We're a nation that believes freedom can never be taken for granted and that each of us has a responsibility to sustain it.

December 6, 2016 *McDill Air Force Base, Tampa, Florida*

November 29, 2016 *President Obama served as a wartime Commander-in-Chief longer than any of his predecessors. Above, during his 23rd visit as President to Walter Reed National Military Medical Center, he does lunges with Lt. Commander John Terry. Commander Terry said he "will remember that until the day I die." (Official White House photo by Pete Souza)*

December 12, 2016 The Daily Show *with Trevor Noah*

2016

The progress we've made has been real and extraordinary.

There's goodness in the majority of people.

The challenge we face today when it comes to race is rarely the overt, Klansman-style of racism ... it's somebody not getting called back for an interview.

December 12, 2016 *Excerpts of President Obama's conversation on race with* The Daily Show's *Trevor Noah*

2016

I want to make sure that I'm doing everything I can to amplify and lift up a next generation of voices not just in politics, but in civic life ... That's where I can be helpful: shine a spotlight on all the great work that's being done and all the wonderful young Americans who will help lead the way.

December 26, 2016 *Excerpt from an interview with David Axelrod on "The Axe Files" podcast*

2016

It is here that we remember that even when hatred burns hottest, the tug of tribalism is at its most primal, we must resist the urge to turn inward. We must resist the urge to demonize those who are different.

Wars can end. The most bitter of adversaries can become the strongest of allies.

As nations, and as people, we cannot choose the history that we inherit. But we can choose what lessons to draw from it, and use those lessons to chart our own futures.

December 27, 2016 *Excerpts of comments at the USS Arizona Memorial in Pearl Harbor, Hawaii*

2017

We have never let go of a belief that has guided us ever since our founding — our conviction that, together, we can change this country for the better. So I hope you'll join me one last time. Because, for me, it's always been about you.

January 2, 2017 *Excerpt of email to supporters announcing a January 10, 2017 farewell speech in Chicago*

2004 - 2017

2017

We have to remember that as we meet the threats of our times, we cannot sacrifice our values or our way of life — the rule of law and openness and tolerance that defines us as Americans. We can't say it enough and we can't show it enough: Thank you for your patriotism. Thank you for your professionalism. Thank you for your character in representing the very best of the American spirit ... It's been a privilege of a lifetime to serve with you.

January 4, 2017 *Farewell to the military at Fort Myer, Virginia*

2017

We have to move forward as we always have: together. That after all, is the story of America, a story of progress. However halting, however incomplete, however harshly challenged at each point on our journey — the story of America is a story of progress. Our best days are still ahead.

January 5, 2017 *Letter to the American public*

2017

We cannot deny the legacy that continues to
drive inequality in how the justice system is experienced
by so many Americans.

January 5, 2017 *Excerpt from the* Harvard Law Review *article*
"The President's Role in Advancing Criminal Justice Reform"

2017

Show up. Dive in. Stay at it. Sometimes you'll win.

Democracy can buckle when we give in to fear. So just as we, as citizens, must remain vigilant against external aggression, we must guard against a weakening of the values that make us who we are.

For all our outward differences, we, in fact, all share the same proud title, the most important office in a democracy: citizen.

Thank you for everything. My last ask is the same as my first: I'm asking you to believe — not in my ability to create change, but in yours.

January 10, 2017 *The President's farewell speech at Chicago's McCormick Place*

WhiteHouse.gov

January 16, 2017 *The World Series Champion Chicago Cubs present Mr. Obama with a "W" flag for the Obama Presidential Center in Chicago.*

Throughout our history, sports has had the power to bring us together even when this country is divided.

It is a game and it is a celebration, but there's a direct line between Jackie Robinson, and me standing here.

Sometimes it's not enough to change laws, you've got to change hearts. And sports has a way, sometimes, of changing hearts that politics or business doesn't.

Remarks at a White House reception for the 2016 Chicago Cubs

2017

Having you in this building has made this place work better. It keeps us honest, it makes us work harder. You have made us think about how we are doing what we do, and whether or not we're able to deliver on what's been requested by our constituents.

I believe in this country. I believe in the American people. I believe that people are more good than bad. I believe tragic things happen. I think there's evil in the world, but I think, at the end of the day, if we work hard and if we're true to those things in us that feel true and feel right, that the world gets a little better each time. That's what this presidency has tried to be about.

January 18, 2017 *Excerpts from the President's final White House news conference*

2017

It is possible —if you're willing to get in the arena — to move history.

The night of the Iowa Caucus was my favorite moment in politics. You could just feel the spirit [of how the democratic process is supposed to work] ... and if you could duplicate that night and that moment across the country and around the world, you felt, at that time, that there wasn't a problem we couldn't solve.

January 18, 2017 *Interview on "Pod Save America" with former Obama aides Jon Favreau, Dan Pfeiffer, Jon Lovett and Tommy Vietor*

2017

This is not a period. This is a comma in the continuing story of building America.

This has been the privilege of my life — I speak for Michelle as well — and we look forward to continuing our journey with all of you. And I can't wait to see what you do next.

I promise you, I'll be right there with you. All right?

January 20, 2017 *Former President Barack Obama gave final remarks at a farewell gathering of staff and supporters at Joint Base Andrews prior to boarding a military aircraft for a flight to Palm Springs, California.*

Library of Congress Control Number: 2017930531

These quotations were curated and edited by publishers Diane Montiel and Steve Alexander, who wish to gratefully acknowledge Beau Rezendes, Ph.D., of Boulder, Colorado. Her shared passion for the project and generosity of time and spirit helped assure that hope, change, optimism and other tenets of the Obama presidency were thoughtfully represented. Thanks, also, to Lindsay Eanet of Chicago, Illinois, for helping proof and copyedit the collection.

The publishers wish to acknowledge Official White House Photographer Pete Souza and his staff, whose thousands of photos chronicling the Obama Administration are archived at *https://obamawhitehouse.archives.gov* and *https://www.flickr.com/photosobamawhitehouse.*

Front cover photograph was taken October 8, 2014, by Pete Souza during a Rose Garden staff meeting.

Back cover photograph was taken July 10, 2014, by Pete Souza as President Obama greeted audience members after delivering remarks on the economy at the Paramount Theatre in Austin, Texas.

Digital drawing in background on page 112 is courtesy of artist Ben Heine: *www.benheine.com*

For more information about the publisher: *www.bantrybaybooks.com*, or email *bantrybaypublishing@gmail.com.*

Coming in Summer 2017 from Bantry Bay Publishing:
"The Quotations of Michelle Obama."

Reader's Guide

The President's quotations are in chronological order.
Many of his themes are indexed below.

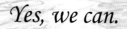

Yes, we can.

November 4, 2008 *Grant Park, Chicago Victory Address*

Yes, we did.

January 10, 2017 *Chicago Farewell Address*